Love Letters from God

Bible Stories

Written by
Glenys Nellist

Illustrated by
Sophie Allsopp

ZONDERkidz

This book is dedicated to the oldest and youngest members of my family.
To my dad, Harry Hughes, who first told me the Story of Jesus.
And to my grandchildren, Xander, Sam, and Brixham, who are just
beginning to hear the wonderful Story for themselves.

His faithfulness continues through all generations. Psalm 100:5

—G.N.

For Charlotte and Silke
with love.
—S.A.

ZONDERKIDZ

Love Letters from God
Copyright © 2014 by Glenys Nellist
Illustrations © 2014 by Sophie Allsopp

This title is also available as a Zondervan ebook.
Visit www.zondervan.com/ebooks.

Requests for information should be addressed to:

Zonderkidz, 3900 Sparks Drive SE, Grand Rapids, Michigan 49546

Library of Congress Cataloging-in-Publication Data

Nellist, Glenys, 1959–
        Love letters from God : Bible stories / Glenys Nellist.
              pages   cm. – (A lift-the-flap book)
        ISBN 978-0-310-73384-3 (hardcover) – ISBN 978-0-310-74260-9 (epub) –
ISBN 978-0-310-74261-6 (epub) – ISBN 978-0-310-74262-3 (epub)
        1. Bible stories, English. 2. Toy and movable books—Specimens. 3. Lift-the-flap books—
Specimens. 4. Board books. I. Title.
BS551.3.N45   2014
220.95'05—dc23   2014010701

All Scripture quotations, unless otherwise indicated, are taken from The Holy Bible, *New
International Reader's Version*®, NIrV®. Copyright © 1995, 1996, 1998 by Biblica, Inc.® Used
by permission. All rights reserved.

Any Internet addresses (websites, blogs, etc.) and telephone numbers in this book are
offered as a resource. They are not intended in any way to be or imply an endorsement by
Zondervan, nor does Zondervan vouch for the content of these sites and numbers for the
life of this book.

All rights reserved. No part of this publication may be reproduced, stored in a retrieval
system, or transmitted in any form or by any means—electronic, mechanical, photocopy,
recording, or any other—except for brief quotations in printed reviews, without the prior
permission of the publisher.

Zonderkidz is a trademark of Zondervan.

Editor: Barbara Herndon
Art direction and design: Jody Langley

Printed in China

18 19 /LPC/ 22 21 20 19 18 17 16 15 14 13 12 11 10 9 8 7 6

Acknowledgments

This book could never have been accomplished alone. My heartfelt thanks belong …

To my brilliant brother, Trevor, who first saw the potential in this book, and with his wit and wisdom helped and encouraged me.

To my best friend, Debi, who shared the dream with me, and whose creativity and love for Christ helped to make the dream come true.

To my children, my biggest cheerleaders … Steven and Natalie; Daniel and Dominique; James and Chelsea; Gareth and Sharon.

To David, my wonderful husband, who stood beside me every step of the way. Without him, this book would never have been completed.

To Crystal Bowman, who helped, mentored, and encouraged me with insight and grace.

And to my colleagues at Zondervan: Doris Rikkers, my invaluable advocate, and Barbara Herndon, my editor, for her patience, wisdom, and guidance.

Finally, to the One who wrote the story before me and without whom there would be no words to share. To Him alone, be the glory.

In the Very Beginning

Creation: Genesis 1

Close your eyes. Can you see the darkness? Did you know that thousands and thousands of years ago, in the very beginning, before God made the world, that's what it was like? Just darkness. Then one magical morning, God said, "Let there be light!" And just like that, the light came. Open your eyes. See the bright wonderful world that God made?

He made everything you can see around you. He made mighty mountains and silver seas. He made green grass and tall trees. He made leopards that leap and eagles that soar. He made bees that buzz and lions that roar.

But there was one thing God made that was better than anything else. One day, God made people. People who could run and jump, people who could laugh and play, people just like you and me.

He made a man named Adam and a woman named Eve, and he gave them a beautiful garden in which to live, called Eden.

For six whole days, God worked really hard making our wonderful world. When God saw everything that he had made, a great big smile spread across his face because he knew that it was all really, really good. And can you guess what he did on the seventh day? He took a great big rest.

Your Love Letter from God

God's Wonderful Words to You

I know the plans I have for you …
I will give you hope for the years to come.
(Jeremiah 29:11)

The Sneaky Snake

Adam and Eve: Genesis 3

In the beautiful Garden of Eden lived a very sneaky snake. He did not like God, and he did not like Adam and Eve. He wanted them out of the garden. So one night, that sneaky snake thought up a very sneaky plan. The next morning, that slimy, sneaky snake slithered up to Eve and quietly whispered in her ear.

"Hello, Eve," he hissed. "Are you hungry this morning? Would you like to try this beautiful, special, shiny apple for breakfast?"

"Why, no!" Eve exclaimed. "Adam and I cannot eat that special, shiny apple. God told us if we eat that fruit, we will have to leave the garden."

"Oh, he didn't really mean that," the sneaky snake replied. "God won't mind if you just take a tiny nibble. This is the tastiest, most delicious fruit in the garden." Eve looked at that special, shiny apple. It looked so good. She smelled that special, shiny apple. It smelled so good. She lifted that special, shiny apple to her mouth and took the tiniest bite. As she handed the apple to Adam, that naughty, sneaky snake laughed and slithered under a bush.

God's Wonderful Words to You

I will not remember your sins anymore.

(Isaiah 43:25)

Oh no! What had Adam and Eve done? As soon as they tasted that fruit, they were so sorry! They knew they had done something very wrong, and now they would have to leave the garden.

Even though they had disobeyed God, he never stopped loving them. They were his children. Even though they had done wrong, he still took care of them. God's love and forgiveness were so much stronger than Adam and Eve's sin. And even though they had to leave the garden, God would never leave them.

Your Love Letter
from God

Noah Needs His Nails

Noah's Ark: Genesis 6–8

Plip plop, plip plop. Was that rain? Noah woke from his sleep and jumped out of bed. Hurrying to the window, Noah peeked out and saw huge gray clouds scurrying toward his house. Noah was ready! For weeks and weeks now, he had been building his big, beautiful boat that God had told him to make. Today was the day he would get to use it. The day when the mighty rains would begin and a flood would cover the whole earth and clean it. Thank goodness Noah had listened to God and made that boat just like God had told him. Now Noah, his family, and all the animals would be safe in the ark. Noah hammered in the last of his nails and then quickly checked his list:

> Two big badgers, two blind bats,
> Two strong camels, and two cute cats.
> Two fast foxes, two fit frogs,
> Two shy deer, and two young dogs.
> Two tall flamingoes, two fat fleas,
> Two black bears, and two small bees ...

Noah's list went on for a long, long time until finally, all the animals were checked in and safely on board.

For forty days and forty nights the rains fell, covering the earth in water. The grass disappeared, the trees disappeared, the mountains disappeared until there was nothing to see except water. In the big boat, Noah was worried. He stood by the window and wondered whether God would remember him. Of course he would! Even though Noah could not see it, God's huge hand was carrying that boat safely until it came to dry ground.

How happy Noah was to be back on land again! All the animals could not wait to get off the ark. Two ran, two hopped, two slithered, two crawled, and two flew ... all in different directions, to find a new home. Noah knelt down to say a thank-you prayer as God painted a rainbow in the sky above. It was, and still is, a wonderful reminder of God's forever love.

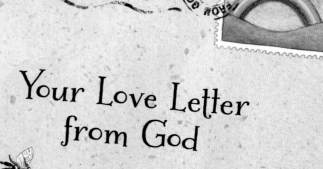

Your Love Letter from God

God's Wonderful Words to You

I have made you. And I will carry you.

(Isaiah 46:4)

The Brave Little Brother

Joseph: Genesis 37–42

Joseph smiled as he hugged his beautiful colored coat. His dad had made that coat for him. Joseph loved the way all the colors sparkled and shimmered in the sun. Pink, purple, red, yellow, gold, brown—his coat was beautiful. Joseph really loved his coat, but his ten older brothers hated it!

"Why does *he* get to have a beautiful coat like that and we don't?" they grumbled. Those ten brothers were so jealous of Joseph and his coat they did something very bad. They stole the coat from Joseph and threw him down a deep, dark well. In the bottom of that deep, dark well, Joseph sat all alone. Except he wasn't alone. God was with him in that dark place.

Suddenly, Joseph's brothers started to pull him out! *Hurrah!* Joseph thought. *Maybe now I can have my coat back and go home.* But that did not happen. Instead, Joseph's cruel brothers sold him to some travelers. Those travelers took Joseph to a strange country, far, far away. But in that strange country, Joseph was not alone. God was still with him.

Can you believe that Joseph had even more troubles? For a long time, he had to work as a slave, doing all kinds of dirty jobs. Then Joseph was thrown in a dark, cold jail for two years. But in the dark, cold jail, Joseph was not alone. God was still with him.

Sometimes, Joseph felt sad about all the bad things that had happened to him. He could not understand how he had lost his beautiful coat, how his brothers could have sold him, how he had been taken far from home, and how people could be so mean to him. But even sitting in that dark, cold jail, Joseph understood one important thing. He had never been alone. God had always been with him.

Do you know what happened to Joseph in the end? One day, Joseph was taken out of that jail. He got a super-duper job working in the king's palace, and most amazing of all, Joseph forgave his brothers. That brave little brother grew up. And God had stayed right with him no matter where he went.

God's Wonderful Words to You

I will never leave you.
(Joshua 1:5)

Your Love Letter
from God

The Little Boy Who Listened

Samuel's Call: 1 Samuel 3:1–10

Candles flickered in the dark rooms. Shadows danced on the walls of the temple where little Samuel lived. It had been a very busy day for him. Samuel had brushed the big wooden floors, cleaned the candlesticks, and polished the plates. Now he was tired and ready for bed. Samuel crawled onto his little mat and pulled his blanket over his head. Suddenly, he heard someone calling his name, "Samuel, Samuel."

Samuel jumped up and ran to Eli's room. What did Eli, the old priest, want at this time of night? But guess what? Eli had not called Samuel at all. Eli was lying down, almost asleep.

"Go back to bed, Samuel," Eli yawned sleepily. "I did not call you."

So Samuel crawled back into his bed. No sooner had his head touched the pillow than he heard that voice a second time. "Samuel, Samuel."

Just like before, Samuel ran to Eli's room, but Eli's reply was the same.

"Go back to bed, Samuel, I did not call you."

So Samuel crawled back into his bed again.

"Samuel, Samuel," the voice came again. This time, little

Samuel threw off his blanket, raced into Eli's room, and shook Eli by the shoulder.

"You must be calling me, Eli. What do you want?" The old priest sat up in bed. He thought for a moment and then looked at the young boy.

"I think *God* is calling you," he said. "If he calls your name again, be sure to tell him you are listening."

And so, an excited Samuel went back to his room and waited. Did God really know his name? He was just a little boy.

Would God call his name again? And into that quiet night came God's voice, softly calling, "Samuel, Samuel."

Samuel immediately sat up in bed and answered, "Hello, God, I am listening."

How happy God was to know that Samuel was a good listener. Now God knew that he could speak to Samuel every day, and every day, Samuel would be listening.

What a wonderful night for Samuel! God knew his name. As the candles flickered and the shadows danced, a happy little Samuel closed his eyes and finally fell asleep.

Your Love Letter from God

God's Wonderful Words to You

I will send for you by name. You belong to me.

(Isaiah 43:1)

David's Day

David's Anointing: 1 Samuel 16:1–13

When Samuel was all grown up, God had a very special job for him to do.

"Samuel," God said, "I want you to go to Jesse's house and ask to see his eight sons. I have chosen one of them to be the next king. When you find him, pour some oil on his head to anoint him, so that everyone will know he is the one I have chosen."

"That's easy," Samuel thought to himself. "I will know the new king right away. He's sure to be tall and handsome, strong and smart. He'll probably be wearing fine, beautiful clothes. I know what a king looks like!"

Sure enough, when Samuel arrived at Jesse's house, out strode Eliab, the eldest son, looking exactly like Samuel had imagined. He was tall and handsome, strong and smart, and he was wearing beautiful clothes that looked like a king's! But just as Samuel was about to anoint Eliab, God gently whispered in Samuel's ear, "No Samuel, he is not the one." Now Samuel was a little confused.

"Are you sure you're not mistaken, God?" Samuel asked. "That young man really did look like a king to me." But God smiled as he replied, "Samuel, I am not looking at how tall, or handsome, or strong he is. I am not looking for someone with fine clothes. I am looking for someone who has a good heart."

So Samuel, who always listened to God, called for the next son, and the next, and the next, to see if he could find which one God had chosen. But even though each one looked like a king to Samuel, the answer was always the same. As the six strong sons marched by, God whispered, "No, no, no, no, no, no."

God's Wonderful Words to You

I have chosen you.
(Isaiah 41:9)

Finally, out came the last, the eighth son. He was just a small boy. He had been working out in the fields, taking care of the sheep, and his clothes were smelly and torn. God gently whispered in Samuel's ear, "Yes, Samuel. Anoint him. He is the one."

And so it was that young David knelt down at Samuel's feet and was anointed with oil in front of his seven brothers. God had chosen David, the shepherd boy, the boy with the good heart. And one day, that little boy would grow up to be a king.

Your Love Letter from God

The Stone That Struck the Giant

David and Goliath: 1 Samuel 17

Goliath was a very ugly, very scary, very big giant. He was as tall as a house. His eyes were as big as baseballs. His legs were as thick as tree trunks. Everyone was afraid of Goliath. Everyone, that is, except little David.

Now David and Goliath were very different. David was small; Goliath was huge. David was quiet; Goliath was noisy. David was kind; Goliath was mean. David sang like a bird; Goliath roared like a lion. David ate porridge for breakfast; Goliath ate squirrels. But the most important difference between David and Goliath was David knew God; Goliath did not.

David knew that God was bigger than Goliath; Goliath thought *he* was bigger than anyone. David knew God was strong; Goliath thought *he* was stronger. David knew when it was time for him to fight that huge giant, God would be fighting with him. Goliath thought that when it was time for him to fight that little boy, *he* could do it alone.

Out onto the battlefield marched Goliath. Out onto the battlefield tiptoed David. "I am going to squash you flat!" roared Goliath in a huge voice.

"My God is so big, so strong, and so mighty," sang David in a quiet voice. Goliath lifted his huge sword. David lifted his small sling. Round and round and round David swung that small sling. Out shot one smooth stone. It flew through the air faster than a speeding bullet. *Kaboom!* It hit Goliath right in the middle of his big forehead. Goliath dropped his huge sword. He rocked backwards and forwards and then fell with a mighty thump to the ground.

Little David ran happily home to have his porridge; Goliath never got to eat another squirrel.

Your Love Letter from God

God's Wonderful Words to You

Do not be afraid. I am with you.

(Isaiah 43:5)

The Lions Who Lost Their Lunch

Daniel in the Lions' Den: Daniel 6

It was an exciting day for the hungry lions as they lay in their den by the king's palace. They had not eaten for days and boy, were they hungry. But today they would get to eat Daniel—the man who was going to be thrown into their den because he would not stop praying to his God. The hungry lions could hardly wait. Their big tummies rumbled as they heard the guards marching with Daniel towards their den. Suddenly, Daniel was falling, falling, falling, down, down, down, into the den. *Bump!* Daniel landed right in front of the hungry lions. Their long whiskers twitched and quivered in delight as they looked at their lunch. Oh my, how good he smelled!

Just then, Daniel rolled over, got to his knees, put his hands together, and closed his eyes. What on earth was he doing? Daniel was talking ever so quietly. Who could he be talking to?

"Dear God," Daniel whispered. "I know you watch over me wherever I go. I know you are watching over me right now. Save me, I pray, from these hungry lions."

The lions almost laughed out loud. So that was it! Daniel was praying to his God! Well, that would do him no good at all. But just as they were about to pounce on Daniel, something strange happened. Suddenly, their big tummies did not feel hungry any more. In fact, they felt quite sleepy. Those big lions closed their big mouths, closed their big eyes, and fell into a deep, deep sleep. And when they woke up the next morning, their lovely lunch was gone. God had saved Daniel after all!

Although the hungry lions lost their lunch that day, they learned an important lesson. They knew, without a doubt, that the God who Daniel loved was watching over all his children—through scary times or happy times, while they were asleep or awake. God was watching over every single one of them every single minute of every single day. And those lions knew that he must be a very wonderful God indeed.

God's Wonderful Words to You

I will watch over you everywhere you go.
(Genesis 28:15)

Your Love Letter
from God

The Very Smelly Belly

Jonah and the Fish: Jonah 1–2

Jonah slowly opened his eyes and tried to figure out where he was. He could hear the sound of gurgling, bubbling water. He could feel something slimy, slippery, and wet under his feet. But it was so dark that he could not see a thing. And what was that smell? It had to be the most disgusting, nasty, horrible fishy smell that Jonah had ever smelled. Where on earth was he? Was he in a cave? No. Was he in a hole? No. Was he in a great big fish? Yes! Jonah was inside the very smelly belly of a very large fish! How on earth had he gotten there? Then, Jonah remembered …

Hadn't God asked Jonah to go to Nineveh, that horrible town, to give the people a message? Hadn't Jonah said no? Hadn't he run away from God and got on board that ship? And when that big storm came, hadn't Jonah jumped overboard? Yes—Jonah remembered now. He fell with an enormous *plop* into that deep, dark, cold water. Then that huge mouth came toward him, swallowing him whole! He was in a great big fish!

What should he do now? Jonah decided he would pray.

Jonah wobbled to his knees, held his nose, and prayed. "Thank you, God, for sending this big fish to rescue me. Thank you for listening to my prayers. I know you can hear me, even though I am in the belly of a fish. Thank you for showing me I should do what you ask—to go to Nineveh and take your message to the people."

Jonah stopped. The smelly belly started to rumble and quake. Suddenly, the fish gave an enormous hiccup. Jonah was catapulted out through the fish's mouth, did several flying somersaults, and landed upside-down on a beach.

Jonah got up, brushed the sand from his knees, peeled away the seaweed that was wrapped around his head, and set off for Nineveh.

God's Wonderful Words to You

You will come and pray to me.
And I will listen to you.
(Jeremiah 29:12)

Bethlehem's Baby Boy

Jesus' Birth: Luke 1

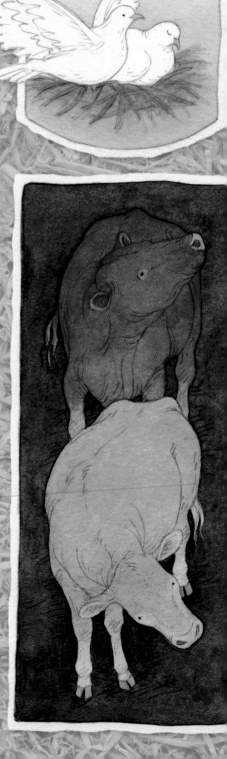

Everything was quiet and still in the town of Bethlehem. In the dark night sky, a single star shone brightly. It peeped into the window of the little stable below to watch all the animals getting ready for bed. The pigeons cooed peacefully in their nest. The mice curled up in the soft hay. The cows nuzzled against each other to keep warm. The donkey closed her eyes. All the animals joined the world of night in a soft, silent sleep.

Suddenly, the stillness was broken by the loud sound of a baby's cry. Up popped the pigeons. Up sprang the mice. Up jumped the cows. Up leapt the donkey. All awakened from their slumber. To their amazement, there was a new baby boy. A beautiful new baby boy, crying and waving his chubby arms and legs as his mom and dad held him up for all the animals to see.

Laughter and song filled the air. The pigeons cooed a chorus. The mice squeaked a melody. The cows mooed to the music. The donkey brayed to the beat. And from the heavens above came the sound of a thousand angels singing—a thousand angels singing to welcome the King of the World, God's one and only Son—Jesus.

And even though the pigeons went back to their nest, even though the mice curled up quietly again, even though the cows returned to their sleep, even though the donkey resumed her rest, and even though baby Jesus slept—the world would never, ever be the same again.

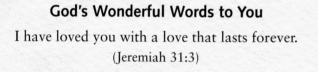

God's Wonderful Words to You

I have loved you with a love that lasts forever.
(Jeremiah 31:3)

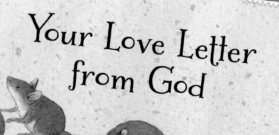

Your Love Letter
from God

The Team of Twelve

Jesus Calls His Disciples: Mark 1:16–20, 2:13–15

Have you ever been hunting for treasure? When Jesus was all grown up, he went hunting for treasure. But he wasn't looking for treasure that sparkles. He wasn't looking for treasure that glitters. He was looking for people. Jesus needed people who would follow him and help tell the world about God. Now if he could find those people, that would be like finding treasure.

The first place Jesus looked for his treasure was at the beach. There, on the shore, he found two fishermen.

"Hello, Peter," Jesus said. "Hello, Andrew." (He knew their names already!) "Will you follow me? Will you do what I do and help me tell the world about God?"

"Yes!" Peter said.

"Yes!" Andrew said.

And right away, they dropped their nets and followed Jesus.

Hurrah! Jesus thought. I have found some treasure!

The next day, Jesus saw Matthew sitting at the market counting his money. I wonder if he will say yes, Jesus thought. And so, he asked him. "Hello, Matthew," Jesus said. "Will you follow me? Will you do what I do and help me tell the world about God?"

"Yes!" Matthew said.

And right away, Matthew dropped his money and followed Jesus.

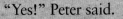

Hurrah! Jesus thought. I have found more treasure!

And so it went. Every day, Jesus looked for people who would follow him. Every day, somebody said yes. How happy Jesus was when he had found his team of twelve. They were his first disciples. That team of twelve really was the very best treasure that Jesus had ever found!

Your Love Letter
from God

God's Wonderful Words to You
You will be my special treasure.
(Exodus 19:5)

The Super-Duper Picnic

Feeding 5,000: John 6

Nathan was *so* excited! He ran along the street with his little picnic basket swinging on his arm. He was going to see Jesus today, and he had a yummy lunch to take with him. Nathan checked his basket. Hiding underneath his picnic blanket were one, two, three, four, five little loaves of bread and two fresh fish. His dad had caught those fish in Lake Galilee that very morning. His picnic was going to taste so good.

Soon, Nathan reached the hillside where Jesus was going to teach everyone. There were a lot of people already there. Grandmas and grandpas, moms and dads, brothers and sisters, aunts and uncles, nieces and nephews. It seemed like every family in the world was there waiting for Jesus. When he spoke, everyone stopped talking and started listening. Even the birds stopped singing so that they could listen. All day long, Nathan sat with the crowd and listened to Jesus. But at the end of the day, everyone started to get hungry. No one had brought any food. No one except Nathan.

"Is there anyone here with a picnic to share?" Jesus asked.

"Well, I could share my five small loaves of bread and two fresh fish," Nathan said. "But I don't think there's enough for everyone."

Jesus gave Nathan a big, wonderful smile that said, "I am pleased with you."

Then, the most amazing thing happened. Jesus took that bread and fish, said thank you to God, and as he passed it around, more and more bread and fish appeared. Every single family on that hillside had some of Nathan's picnic. Every grandma and grandpa, every mom and dad, every sister and brother, every aunt and uncle, every niece and nephew. Everyone had enough to eat. It was a miracle!

As Nathan ran home with his empty basket, he was so glad he had shared his lunch. Just think, Jesus had taken Nathan's five little loaves and his two fresh fish and turned them into a super-duper picnic. It had been a meal that Nathan would never, ever forget!

God's Wonderful Words to You

I am pleased with you.
(Exodus 33:17)

GOD
xoxo

Wind and Waves

Storm on the Lake: Mark 4:35–41

It was a beautiful day on Lake Galilee. Golden sunlight danced on the water. A gentle breeze whispered softly in the air.

Small waves rippled quietly across the water. In the little boat, the disciples rested after a busy day's work. Jesus put his head on a comfy cushion and closed his eyes. All was peaceful, quiet, and calm.

Then, as if from nowhere, great gray clouds marched across the sky and pushed the sun out of the way. The gentle breeze turned into a mighty rushing wind. Those small rippling waves became big, bouncing waters. In the little boat, the disciples were scared. What was happening? An enormous clap of thunder boomed above, and the heavens opened as a bolt of lightning streaked down toward the little boat. Now the disciples were terrified! Their little boat rocked up and down as the mighty waves jumped over the deck. They were going to drown! Where was Jesus? Surely he could save them!

Above the noise of the storm, the disciples thought they heard another, quieter sound. That couldn't possibly be the sound of someone snoring, could it? But it was! Jesus was fast asleep on that comfy cushion, and he was snoring—snoring while that mighty storm was raging all around them!

"Jesus! Jesus!" the disciples cried. "Save us, save us!"

Jesus woke up, stood in that little boat, and held his hand out over the raging waters. He said two tiny words:

"Be still."

And an amazing thing happened. Those crashing, thundering waters became small waves again. That mighty, rushing wind turned back into a gentle breeze. Those great gray clouds scurried away and the sun slid back where it belonged. The storm had stopped.

The disciples were amazed. Who was this man who could calm the wind and stop the waves? This man was Jesus, the Son of God.

God's Wonderful Words to You

I will take hold of your hand.

(Isaiah 42:6)

Your Love Letter from God

The Little Lost Lamb

The Lost Sheep: Luke 15

There was once a good shepherd who had one hundred sheep. He loved each of his sheep very much and knew all of their names. Every day, he would lead them to green pastures where they could eat the best fresh grass. On their way home, he would lead them to still, cool waters where they could drink. Every evening, at bedtime, the good shepherd would count his sheep to make sure they were all safely in their pen.

One night, the shepherd began to count his sheep … 90, 91, 92, 93, 94, 95, 96, 97, 98, 99—Oh no! Little Fluffy was missing! Now what do you suppose the good shepherd did? Did he lie down and go to sleep, hoping that Fluffy would come back the next day? No! Did he say to himself, "Oh well, never mind, I still have 99 sheep"? No! Did he sit down and cry? No! He got right up and went out to search for his little lost lamb.

God's Wonderful Words to You

You are the sheep
belonging to my flock.
(Ezekiel 34:31)

Your Love Letter
from God

That good shepherd marched back through the meadows, hiked over the hills, and splashed through the streams. He burrowed under the bushes, thrashed through the thicket, and fought his way around the forests, shouting, "Fluffy, Fluffy, where are you?" Then, he heard the faintest little cry, "Baa, baa, baa."

"Fluffy!" the shepherd cried as he happily scooped her up into his arms. "I'm so glad I found you!"

And with his heart full of love, the good shepherd lifted her ever so gently, put her high on his shoulders, and carried her carefully all the way back home. Fluffy nuzzled her head into his warm, strong shoulder and decided that she would never, ever leave the good shepherd again.

The Tiny Tax Collector

Zacchaeus: Luke 19:1–10

In the town of Jericho lived a tiny tax collector named Zacchaeus. More than anything else in the whole world, Zacchaeus loved money. He loved to touch it. He loved to smell it. He really loved to count it. The trouble was Zacchaeus was greedy. When he collected taxes from the people, he took much more than he should have. Because of that, Zacchaeus had no friends. But what did it matter if Zacchaeus had no friends? He had money! For Zacchaeus, having money was the only thing that really mattered.

God's Wonderful Words to You

I have called you friends.
(John 15:15)

Your Love Letter
from God

One day, Jesus came to Jericho. Zacchaeus ran down the street, hoping to get a glimpse of Jesus, but the crowd would not let him through. Try as he might, Zacchaeus could not see over their heads. That tiny tax collector stood on the very tips of his toes, but he couldn't see Jesus. That tiny tax collector jumped as high as he could, but he still couldn't see Jesus. So do you know what Zacchaeus did? He climbed a tall sycamore tree. Now he could see Jesus. And Jesus could see him!

"Zacchaeus," Jesus called. "Come down. I would like to come to your house today." Zacchaeus could not believe his tiny ears. Oh no! Suppose Jesus found out that Zacchaeus was greedy?

Suppose Jesus found out that Zacchaeus took far too much money from people? What would happen when they talked?

Something utterly amazing.

Zacchaeus changed! After Jesus talked with him, Zacchaeus was not greedy anymore. In fact, he gave back all the money he owed and more. Zacchaeus discovered that he loved Jesus much more than money. Zacchaeus loved to talk to Jesus, and Zacchaeus really loved to listen to Jesus. And in the end, for Zacchaeus, having Jesus as his very best friend was the only thing that really mattered.

Remember Me

The Last Supper: Luke 22:14–20

Jesus sat and looked at the long table where he would eat supper with his disciples. A lovely large loaf of warm, crusty bread sat in the middle of the table. It filled the whole room with a delicious smell. Next to it stood a tall pitcher filled to the brim with fresh, cool wine. Everything was ready.

Jesus looked at his precious team of twelve disciples as they sat around the table. They had been so good to him. They had followed Jesus wherever he went. They had told so many people about God. Jesus was going to miss them a lot.

Jesus knew that he had nearly finished his work on earth. Jesus knew that even though he had done nothing wrong, there were still some people who hated him. Jesus knew that soon,

those same people would hang him on a big, heavy, wooden cross and leave him there to die. But although Jesus felt sad about that, he felt happy that he had been able to show so many people just how much God loved them.

Jesus would never forget how God helped him feed 5,000 people. He would never forget how God helped him calm a great big storm on Lake Galilee. Most of all, Jesus would never forget his wonderful disciples. But would his disciples forget him? Jesus didn't want that. So he decided to make their last supper together very special.

Jesus picked up that warm, crusty loaf of bread, broke it, and gave a piece to each of his disciples. As they ate it, Jesus

God's Wonderful Words to You

I will not forget you.
(Isaiah 49:15)

softly whispered, "Whenever you eat some bread, I want you to remember me."

Then Jesus picked up that tall pitcher of wine and poured some out for each of his disciples. As they each took a sip, Jesus softly whispered, "Whenever you have a drink, I want you to remember me."

What a special supper. After that, every time those disciples ate some bread, guess who they remembered? Jesus! And every time they had a drink, guess who they remembered? Jesus!

Those disciples never forgot Jesus, and Jesus never, ever forgot them.

Your Love Letter
from God

The Saddest Story

The Crucifixion: Luke 23:23–49

Jesus was sad and scared and lonely and tired. He slowly carried his big, heavy, wooden cross up to the top of the hill. And when he reached the top, the soldiers took that big, heavy, wooden cross and nailed him to it. They hammered nails through his hands. They hammered nails through his feet. They laughed at him and called him names. Then they lifted that big, heavy, wooden cross. They stood it up and left him hanging there.

Suddenly, the birds stopped singing. The sun stopped shining. The flowers hung their heads. Darkness crept in without a sound and covered the world in its deep, silent shadow. Jesus closed his eyes. And then with a roar, the whole earth shook. The mighty mountains trembled. And God's tears fell like raindrops from the sky. It was the day that his Son, his one and only Son, Jesus, died.

Your Love Letter from God

God's Wonderful Words to You

I will see you again. Then you will be full of joy.

(John 16:22)

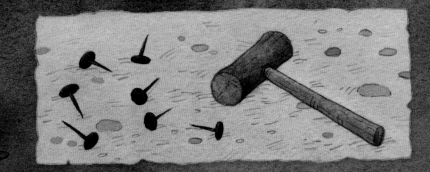

The Happy Ending!

The Resurrection: John 20:1–18

Three days later, the early morning sun tried to peek through the clouds as Jesus' friend Mary came up the hillside to put perfume on Jesus' body. Quietly, she tiptoed up to the big cave where they had buried him. Suddenly, she stopped. Something was wrong. The great big stone that had covered the doorway was gone. Who could have moved that heavy stone? Mary slowly peered inside the dark cave. She could not believe what she saw. Jesus was gone! Who had taken his body? Where had they put him? Mary began to cry, but then, she heard a voice behind her.

"Why are you crying?" a man asked.

"Oh please, sir," Mary sobbed. "Are you the gardener? Someone has taken my Jesus away. If you know where he is, can you tell me?"

"Mary," the man whispered.

Mary's heart skipped a beat. How did this man know who she was? How could his voice sound so much like Jesus as he softly whispered her name? Mary blinked through her tears at the man standing in front of her. Could it really be true? Was this man Jesus? Was Jesus alive again? And suddenly, she knew it was him!

The sun jumped out from behind the clouds, the birds began to sing again. The flowers in the fields lifted their heads as they danced in the wind. The whole earth seemed to shout his name. *Jesus! Jesus! Jesus was alive!* And from the heavens up above came the sound of a thousand angels singing—a thousand angels singing to welcome back Jesus—Jesus, the King of the World!

Mary's heart sang for joy! If Jesus could live again, even after he had died, that meant one day, Mary could live again too! And if Jesus would have a new home in heaven, that meant one day, Mary would have a new home in heaven too!

With a hop, a skip, and a jump Mary ran to tell the disciples. Jesus was alive! Jesus was alive, and one day, one wonderful day, Mary would be able to live in heaven with Jesus forever.

God's Wonderful Words to You

Because I live, you will live also.
(John 14:19)

Your Love Letter
from God

Your Invitation

God's Wonderful Words to You

And you can be sure
that I am always with you.
(Matthew 28:20)